A Day on the **Farm**

FIRST EDITION
Project Editor Mary Atkinson; **Art Editor** Susan Calver; **Senior Editor** Linda Esposito;
Deputy Managing Art Editor Jane Horne; **US Editor** Regina Kahney; **Production** Kate Oliver;
Picture Researcher Jo Carlill; **Illustrator** Norman Young;
Reading Consultant Linda Gambrell, PhD

THIS EDITION
Editorial Management by Oriel Square
Produced for DK by WonderLab Group LLC
Jennifer Emmett, Erica Green, Kate Hale, *Founders*

Editors Grace Hill Smith, Libby Romero, Michaela Weglinski;
Photography Editors Kelley Miller, Annette Kiesow, Nicole DiMella;
Managing Editor Rachel Houghton; **Designers** Project Design Company;
Researcher Michelle Harris; **Copy Editor** Lori Merritt; **Indexer** Connie Binder;
Proofreader Larry Shea; **Reading Specialist** Dr. Jennifer Albro; **Curriculum Specialist** Elaine Larson

Published in the United States by DK Publishing
1745 Broadway, 20th Floor, New York, NY 10019

Copyright © 2023 Dorling Kindersley Limited
DK, a Division of Penguin Random House LLC
23 24 25 26 27 10 9 8 7 6 5 4 3 2 1
001–333434–Apr/2023

A catalog record for this book
is available from the Library of Congress.
HC ISBN: 978-0-7440-6705-7
PB ISBN: 978-0-7440-6706-4

DK books are available at special discounts when purchased
in bulk for sales promotions, premiums, fundraising, or
educational use. For details, contact: DK Publishing Special Markets,
1745 Broadway, 20th Floor, New York, NY 10019
SpecialSales@dk.com

Printed and bound in China

The publisher would like to thank the following for their kind permission to reproduce their images:
a=above; c=center; b=below; l=left; r=right; t=top; b/g=background
Dorling Kindersley: Peter Chadwick / Natural History Museum, London 13cra, 30tl; **Dreamstime.com:** Chanidapha
Charoensuk 16b, Charles Brutlag 15cr, Clara Bastian 16-17, Sue Feldberg 12; **Shutterstock.com:** Danita Delimont 6,
Michael O'Reilly 29, Manasa Qaranivalu 4-5, Kuttelvaserova Stuchelova 15cl

Cover images: *Front:* **Shutterstock.com:** Svitlana Holovei;
Back: **Shutterstock.com:** Ekaterina_Mikhaylova, aliaksei kruhlenia cra
All other images © Dorling Kindersley

For the curious
www.dk.com

A Day on the
Farm

Sue Nicholson

Contents

Time to Wake Up

It is early in the morning.
The farm is quiet.

Then, the rooster begins to crow.

What a noise!

Cock-a-doodle-doo!

He wakes up all the other farm animals.

In the barn, the mother hen starts to cluck.

One of her eggs is ready to hatch.

Cluck
Cluck

Peck, peck, peck!
A tiny chick breaks
through its shell.

shell

More eggs crack open.
Five cheeping chicks
hatch out!

Cheep Cheep
Cheep Cheep

Other farm babies hatch from eggs, too.

The mother duck has six ducklings.

Quack
Quack

The mother goose has
four goslings.

Honk
Honk

The ducks waddle down to the pond. They take a morning dip.

Their wide, webbed feet push them through the water.

The ducklings have soft, fluffy feathers called "down."

down

Quack

Soon, they will grow long, oily feathers to keep them warm and dry.

Geese like to be near
water, too.
The mother goose snaps
up grass and weeds
in her bright orange bill.

She flaps her wings
and honks if anyone
comes near her goslings.

Honk

Time for Lunch

The cows come to the gate. It is time for milking!

The farmer milks the cows. The farmer will sell the milk for people to drink.

The cows go back
to the field
to munch grass.

Munch

Munch

17

Other animals
are hungry, too.

A sheep is
nibbling hay.

So is a goat.

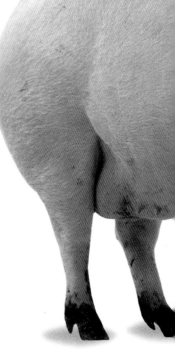

The pigs
root around
for food
in the barn.

One pig has her snout
in a bucket of corn!

snout

The farm babies tell their mothers that they are hungry.

"Baa, baa!" cries the lamb to the mother sheep.

Baa
Baa

"Naa, naa!" cries the kid to the mother goat.

Naa

Naa

The piglets squeal. They drink their mother's milk.

Playtime

Baby animals love to play. The kids butt each other with their horns.

horns

The piglets
like to roll
in the mud.

Out in the fields, the lambs skip and jump. Skip, hop, jump! One tiny hoof follows another.

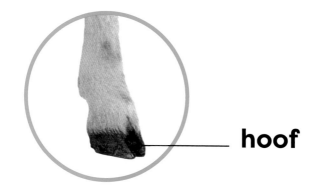

hoof

One calf has lost his mother. "Moo! Moo!" he calls. The mother cow calls back. She is not far away.

Moo
Moo

Woof

In the afternoon, the sheepdog helps the farmer round up the sheep.

Then, the farmer cuts the wool off the sheep.

The sheep look smaller and cleaner without their wool.

Baa
Baa

wool

Evening comes. It is dark.
The farm is quiet.

The chicks, the lambs,
and the piglets fall
fast asleep.

Zzzzzzz

Zzzzzzz

Zzzzzzz

The cat will keep watch until the rooster crows again.

Glossary

down
the small fluffy feathers that keep a bird warm

hoof
the hard part of the foot of some animals

horns
the curved and pointed hard parts on some animals' heads

snout
the long extended nose part of some animals

wool
the thick, soft, curly fur of a sheep or goat

Index

Quiz

Answer the questions to see what you have learned. Check your answers with an adult.

1. What is a gosling?

2. Why do farmers milk cows?

3. How do piglets like to play?

4. What does the sheepdog do on the farm?

5. Which farm animal is your favorite? What does that animal eat and do at the farm?

1. A baby goose 2. To sell the milk for people to drink
3. They roll in the mud 4. Helps the farmer round up the sheep
5. Answers will vary